DREAMER'S DREAM

AUTHOR, JULIE MCCULL[...]
ILLUSTRATOR, VALENTINA TAL[...]

This Book Belongs to…

There once was a dream of a baby, a dream that a baby was here.

All the dreamers helped grow the tummy, strong throughout every day.

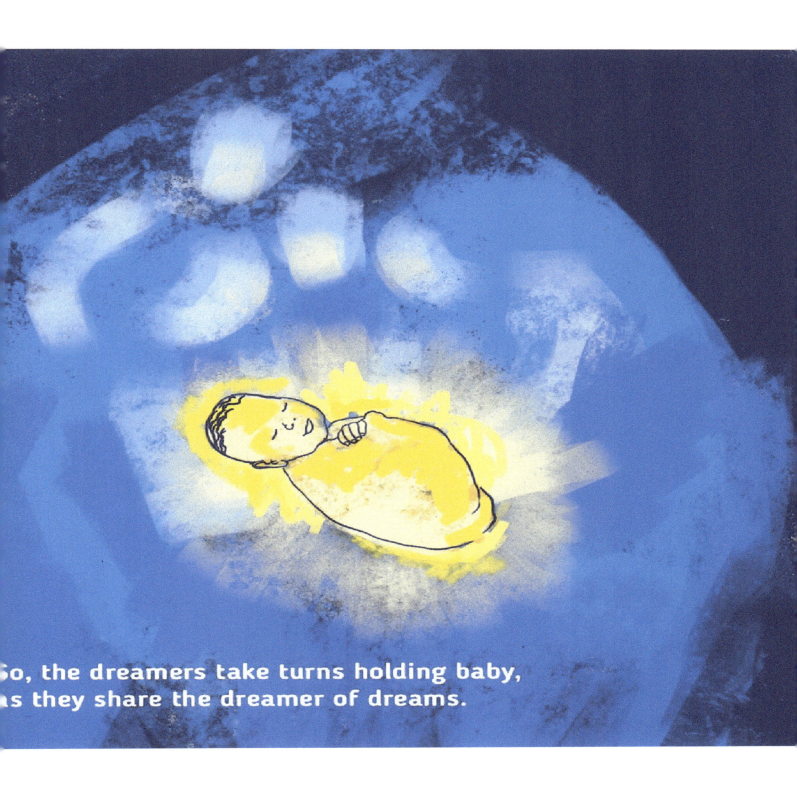

So, the dreamers take turns holding baby,
as they share the dreamer of dreams.

"Forever, Always, and so much..."
to the baby they whisper and sing.

"What can we name this baby?"
The dreamers wondered out loud,

All the dreamers help nurture the baby,
No matter how big or how small.

They all play a part, teach love from the heart,
Come together and show love from all.

Dreamer's Dream is a book written in HOPE to strengthen happy homes. Write beautiful memories about you're birthing experience Or write your children's reactions and sweet comments to remember forever.

★ Suggested questions and topics! ★

★ Did you have people helping you through the pregnancy? ★

★ Did you have a large support group by your side? ★

★ Were you the one pregnant or was there a surrogate/birth mom? ★

★ What was the day you or you're surrogate went into labor like? ★

★ Who held baby first, second, and third? ★

★ Where does your babies name originate from? ★

★ Have you had more babies? What are their stories if so? ★

★ Did you have a large support group by your side? ★

★ Were you the one pregnant or was there a surrogate/birth mom? ★

★ How long did you wish for your babies? ★

★ How long did you wish for your babies? ★

★ Was it challenging to become pregnant? ★

★ Did you have people helping you through the pregnancy? ★

★ Did you have a large support group by your side? ★

★ Were you the one pregnant or was there a surrogate/birth mom? ★

★ What was the day you or you're surrogate went into labor like? ★

★ Who held baby first, second, and third? ★

★ Where does your babies name originate from? ★

★ Have you had more babies? What are their stories if so? ★

★ Did you have a large support group by your side? ★

★ Were you the one pregnant or was there a surrogate/birth mom? ★

What is your story?

What is your story?

_____
_____
_____
_____
_____
_____
_____
_____
_____
_____
_____

★

What is your story?

What is your story?

What is your story?

★ *Dreamer's Dream* ★

A message from the Author,

This book can relate to single parents, families of 2 or more parents, and adoption. This children's book helps open deep and important conversations with your little ones about your unique and beautiful family dynamic. Read to your child/children about how much you hoped and dreamed for them, how special they are, and how it can take a village to bring a dream come true. The beautiful illustration in this book is sure to capture the eye and a give a great visual.

- Julie McCullough

CPSIA information can be obtained
at www.ICGtesting.com
Printed in the USA
LVHW071228210321
681561LV00055B/459